THE
DEFINITIVE GUIDE
TO **MAKING MONEY ONLINE** WITH
YOUR WRITING

THE DEFINITIVE GUIDE TO MAKING MONEY ONLINE WITH YOUR WRITING

CLARK R. COVINGTON

Copyright © 2008 by Clark Covington. All rights reserved.

Two Harbors Press
212 3rd Avenue North, Suite 570
Minneapolis, MN 55401
612.455.2293
www.TwoHarborsPress.com

All rights reserved. No part of this publication may be reproduced, stored in a retrieval system, or transmitted, in any form or by any means, electronic, mechanical, photocopying, recording, or otherwise, without the written prior permission of the author.

ISBN - 978-1-935097-01-3
ISBN - 1-935097-01-6
LCCN - 2008904913

Book sales for North America and international:
Itasca Books, 3501 Highway 100 South, Suite 220
Minneapolis, MN 55416
Phone: 952.345.4488 (toll free 1.800.901.3480)
Fax: 952.920.0541; email to orders@itascabooks.com

Cover Design by Wes Moore
Typeset by Peggy LeTrent

Printed in the United States of America

Contents

Introduction 7

Chapter One
Web Content 11

Chapter Two
E-Books 17

Chapter Three
SEO Article Writing 28

Chapter Four
Sales Letter Writing 37

Chapter Five
Press Release Writing 47

Chapter Six
Autoresponder and Email Writing 56

Chapter Seven
Blogs 62

Chapter Eight
Newsletter Writing and Design 66

Chapter Nine
A Few Other Jobs 72

Conclusion 75

About the Author 77

Introduction

Welcome to the wonderful world of online freelance writing, where the conventional rules of writing for profit are tossed out the door. The days of needing advanced degrees and intelligent-looking glasses to be taken seriously have been replaced by savvy stay-at-home moms and independent-minded entrepreneurs. The goal of these individuals is not to become millionaires or rule the freelance writing landscape, but rather to make a few extra bucks for the luxuries of life, such as a flat screen TV or eating out on the weekends. Or, maybe they need the money for more serious purposes, such as taking care of a sick relative. Either way, online freelance writing can be a great way to achieve your financial objectives through a variety of interesting, and often educational work.

Growing up in a small town full of brilliant people, I seemed to play second fiddle to those who were more advantaged academically. They would always achieve perfect scores on their SATs or they had an opportunity to spend their summers taking special courses at Ivy League universities. In fact, they were so smart that they helped my high school achieve a special honor. In 1998 my school, (Bronxville High School), was rated by Newsweek as one of the top 10 high schools in the country for academics.

Reflecting back on all of that, it is no wonder why I slipped through the cracks. Granted, I never finished last in the class, but I was not very close to the first either. This cycle extended into my college years at Ohio Wesleyan University. During this time my academic career was marred with mediocre grades and a somewhat disappointing 2.5 GPA at graduation.

How then did I become what some have proclaimed the foremost expert on freelance writing online? How I have been able to dominate several markets of online freelance writing when I myself am not the most academically inclined individual? How is it that I have built a team of over 300 writers that have helped me to become the source for a large part of the content produced online today? The answer is simple; the Internet has opened new doors for people like me, you, and anybody else that can type a few pages of text.

One of the most notable components of any website on the Internet is the written word. An incidental part of the massive and explosive growth of the Internet has been the need for quality writing on websites. It does not take long for website owners interested in gaining more traffic and sales to realize that good, conversational-style writing is a must in this business.

This is where you come in. This is where I come in. This is where we meet to make money. The Internet has allowed people of all abilities to create content for websites in massive amounts for subjects as diverse as dog grooming accessories to swimwear collections.

I have personally had the opportunity to work with companies as large as Lending Tree and as small SEC Sports Fan, a SEC sports forum operated by just one person. Through my work with hundreds of clients, I have experienced a wealth of incredible knowledge that I hope to pass on to you in this book.

Another side of my business that I personally care the most about, is my ever growing team of writers. With over 300 writers on staff, I have seen the amazing happen time and time again. I have seen a blind lady write about corsets and lingerie. I have seen a woman with MS write about bridal accessories. I have seen a Christian missionary write about taxes, and a stay-at-home mom write about football games. In short, I have seen a lot of people do great things, which has prompted me to write this book.

I figured if they could write and get paid for their content, often with their backs up against the wall with fulltime jobs and families to balance, then why can't you? Why can't you become the next writer to make money for your written word? I believe you can, which is why I wrote this book.

The following information will inform you on the absolute best ways to make money online through your writing. These methods are neither quick nor easy. They are also not too good to be true, since they still involve a lot of hard work. But for those willing to put in the effort and keep an open mind, a nice income awaits them.

Thanks for taking the time out of your day to read this. Without further delay, let's get you on your way to online profits through freelance writing.

Chapter 1
Web Content

Companies are often dumbfounded when it comes to writing their own web content. The concept for the website is outsourced to the website design firm, and somewhere along the line the firm lets the company know they aren't writers. This is when they suggest that their client hire a freelance writer to complete the content that will compliment the site's design. An occurrence similar to the one above jumpstarted my web content writing career several years ago.

At a time in my life when money was absolutely an issue, writing articles for eight dollars each was starting to wear on me. The once budding freelance writer was now a down trodden, overworked grump. I had dozens of assignments coming in, yet they all were low paying, and required scrupulous attention to detail. I was, in short, yearning for something else… something better.

Vertical Measures, a SEO firm that I had been doing keyword articles for, needed some site content done for their new website. The company had the design completed, and simply needed someone to write about their various services, and unique approach to search engine optimization. While I was still green as a freelance writer, I knew from reading other people's experiences online that web content writing paid a higher fee. I was able to negotiate a contract of about $400 for around 14 pages of writing. This was nearly triple my normal pay for writing keyword based articles, and would be a good addition to my portfolio. So, I took the job.

After several days of writing feverishly, and researching some of the concepts that I was to write about, the project was coming to completion. After going through several phases of revisions, the project was finished, and I was paid in full. For the first time in my young life as a writer, I had made more than $10 per page. Boy, did it feel damn good!

To this day web content remains a major untapped market. I have worked on dozens of web content projects, regularly bidding upwards of $80 to $100 per page. The projects typically can be done in two to three days time. Also, the writing is often stimulating and challenging, making it a wonderful specialty for those interested in getting paid the most money per word written.

Definition

Web content is typically categorized as the pages of a website. Examples include: the homepage, the FAQ, about us and contact us pages. Web content is often outsourced by smaller companies that do not employ a copywriter on the staff. Web content can also include long-form direct mail style sales letters, and survey-style questions for visitors to answer.

Modes of Acquisition

Coming upon web content jobs is easier than most would assume. These high-paying jobs are readily available on various freelance job boards such as Elance.com and Guru.com. I have, for reasons unbeknown to me, acquired the most web content jobs from Guru.com. However, there have been plenty of jobs up for bid on Elance.com as well as through private email leads generated from my website.

To best achieve web content related jobs, a calculated approach is recommended. For starters be sure to create a website, or at the very least an email-friendly file that profiles samples of web content you have produced. If you are just starting out, try creating a website concept on a topic you have knowledge on, and then writing out the basic 5 pages of a website. This would be the homepage, the about us, the FAQ, the contact us and a page with product or service information. This exercise will not only sharpen your writing skills, it will also provide a realistic sample of your work to possible clients.

Armed with at least 1 sample of your work, you are ready to approach the freelance boards to bid on projects. This is a great way to limit the cost of acquiring a project by simply paying the fee to bid on web content related projects, and making your bid as compelling as possible.

For those that are more interested in making the bulk of their work web content related, creating a website might work best. There are very few companies that sell web content related services online via a dedicated website, and those that do are typically confusing hard to navigate websites that almost force the buyer to leave without purchasing. For an example of a basic website that converts fairly well for web content, visit my site www.WebCopywritingService.com and feel free to use it as inspiration for your own site.

WHAT TO EXPECT IN TERMS OF PAY

In order to attract the highest quality jobs, you must establish your per page rate for web content writing. For companies that want excellent writing, the per page rate in my experience should be no lower than $30. The higher end is up to you, but I would start out quoting around $40 to $60 per page for a web content assignment of 5 to 10 pages. For example, say a potential client posted a project on a freelance board for web content of 7 pages. Let's further suppose this content is supposed to be about a new site selling state-of-the-art music software that organized and played MP3s on your computer. My quote would be around $350 to $500 for the project. I would include unlimited revisions, and updates in the quote. This project, depending on your available time to focus, would take about an hour per page to write, at least if you're familiar with the subject. This would net your pay somewhere around $40 per hour, which wouldn't be too bad for most freelance writers. It would also have you come well under the $100 per page rate that many established writers will charge.

TIPS FOR GETTING THE JOB DONE QUICKLY AND EFFICIENTLY

After landing the dream web content project, the euphoria of your victory will quickly turn into fear and anxiety if you are not prepared to actually produce the content in a timely, organized and well thought out manner. To help you keep sane, and provide you with a step-by-step look at how to get web content projects done, I have outlined my personal method below.

Start with outlining how many pages need to be completed. This can be done by simply writing out on a notepad, or typing out on the computer the page titles for each page that needs to be done. Once this is finished, list out under each page title what information the client would like you to include. For example, under the homepage title, you would include a cue to write about the client's unique traits that make them the leader in their market. You would also write a cue to discuss the client's excellent track record in their respective market, etc.

It is not unusual for a client to list out the cues he or she would like you to write about in an email to you. Some clients will call on the phone and gab it to your ear like you have a memory that will never forget their intricate company details. For those clients it is important to urge them to write out what they want in an email. It is extremely important for you to have their needs in writing, as it will serve as the core or foundation for your writing, and often will eliminate several rounds of revisions that would occur from missing something the client wanted.

If the client does not provide a detailed list of what they want on each web content page, it is necessary to come up with a draft of what you think they would want. Once you have a draft, email it to them. Or, if they are in the Stone Age, fax them a copy, and then setup a time to discuss the project on the phone.

Once you have a cue list of what each page in the project should include, it is time to start writing. Even for technical topics, I would advise you to start writing first, and it will best uncover the points in the web content that might require more research to come to fruition.

At this point the production should be fairly simple. Write, revise, send over to the client for approval and finish up. Depending on the scope of the project, most web content assignments can be completed in a week or less, and often net repeat business when the client has a new website that needs that witty, thought provoking written word only you can provide.

Disadvantages

In my experience the most cumbersome problem with writing web content is getting paid. It is highly advised to require full payment up front. I have had several clients barter the cost of services provided post project. Since the writing was already completed, it was not a negotiation I would advise anyone to take part in. The leverage is entirely in the client's favor since the writing has already been done, and effectively useless to you if you are not paid by the client in advance.

Also, revisions are more prevalent in web content. Most of your clients will have a particular vision for the finished project, and if your work is not in line with their vision, even if it is remarkably well done, will require revisions. Sending a writing cue list in advance will help curb this issue to some extent, but it is still advised that you quote the client a rate that allows you to be comfortable with doing multiple revisions throughout the life of the job.

Future Opportunities

The current market for web content projects is booming. There are more people in need of quality, reasonably priced, web content than there are providers. PR and Advertising firms are also prime candidates for ghostwriting web content jobs.

As long as there are websites being made there will be a need for web content. The proliferation of high speed Internet and computer access in countries around the world has increased the need for proficient English writers to develop web content.

Out of five stars, this particular element of online freelance writing gets four. It is absolutely open for new writers to enter the market, and has the potential to be profitable for the right provider.

Becoming an Industry Leader

Dominating the web content market is attainable, and can even be likely if the marketing and pitch was in line with demand. Up to this point the Internet has not seen a company offer web content at reasonable rates to the masses. Researching comparable markets like website design or search engine optimization can help you come up with a marketing/positioning plan to be the provider of web content to webmasters in need.

Niche markets are also available for domination. Specializing in creating web content for a certain field should lead to higher per page rates, and greater opportunities for referrals. Imagine being the preferred web content writer for real estate agents across the country. Last time I checked, that position has yet to be filled, which helps to illustrate just how wide open the web content writing market is.

Chapter 2
E-books

Writing an e-book can be a rewarding experience in a number of ways. Publishing an e-book is as quick as clicking the save button on your word processor. The editing process is what you make it, and the community of e-book buyers is growing by the day. For me, writing an e-book literally changed my life. It was one of those experiences that took me totally by surprise in a time that was filled with turmoil.

Living in South Carolina has its advantages and disadvantages. Serious advantages would include beautiful beaches, stunning women, (like the one I've been dating for four years), kind people and affordable housing.

Disadvantages to living in South Carolina are primarily focused around two things: the heat and the lackluster job market. With a Bachelors Degree from a place some have called the Harvard of the Midwest, Ohio Wesleyan University, and a Masters Degree from the University of South Carolina in English with an emphasis in Speech Communications, you would think my chances at landing a job would be good, if not great.

The heat in South Carolina is bearable in the winter, but can become somewhat extraordinary in the summers. If life is not going your way, the South Carolina heat has a way of making the pain magnify, something akin to baking the pain slowly into your soul.

After spending my first three years living in South Carolina attending graduate school and teaching, I figured I would test the job market to see what other jobs were available. I should note that shortly after graduate school I tried my hand at owning a retail clothing store, which was a tremendous failure. It netted me a great financial loss, incredible amounts of personal debt, and about 30 lbs of weight gained directly to my gut. Whoever said retail was a tough profession, forgot to mention the industry's ability to suck the life out of a person in ways never before thought possible. I still fiddle with fashion related endeavors, however I remain very aware of just how challenging that field of business can be.

As you might have guessed, by this point life was not going so well for me. The summer of 2006 was a difficult one. I could not find a job, even with all my degrees and availability. I was willing to work anytime anybody needed anything, yet still had trouble finding a decent job.

On top of the job problem I had mounting personal debt from the failed retail store. My teaching career consisted of teaching a few night courses at a local college for enough money to pay the rent, and a few of my many bills. For the first time in my life the negative was starting to outweigh the positive.

It was early July and I had finished teaching a night class, and had just about had it with teaching. The pay was lousy and the students were tired since this class ran to 9 pm on Friday nights. I mean, who wants to learn about the history of public speaking on a Friday night in a small hot room in a generic office building for 3 hours? The stress was staring to really take its toll.

After coming home from class, I decided to do something I had never done before… write an e-book. I had been secretly studying the art of Internet marketing for several months with no success. I had followed a trail left by a freelance client to the center of the Internet marketing world, known to many experienced marketers as the Warrior Forum. The Warrior Forum is a website that discusses what I like to call the raw aspect of Internet marketing. Everything is covered on the forum from the tools necessary to market on the Internet, to the vast and somewhat tacky history of the Internet marketing profession. One part fascinating, one part distributing, getting into the minds of the those in the online marketing trenches can really shed light on how to run a successful business on the Internet.

Yes, if you did not know it already, there are thousands, if not hundreds of thousands of people around the world that make their living marketing stuff online. What was once reserved for shady affiliate marketing and pyramid schemes has now become one of the most lucrative places in the world to market a product or service. Internet marketing is in fact where I credit my ultimate successes as a writer, and business owner. For this part in the story, however, it is just important to understand that the core, or pulse of the Internet marketing community gathers at the Warrior Forum, and that is where I cut my teeth writing an e-book that would eventually change my life forever.

Tired and disheartened, I decided to just write my e-book one Friday night. Several months earlier I had purchased an online business from an eBay auction with $1,100 from my tax refund, hoping for a miracle. The business served the owners of online forums by posting relevant content on their message boards. I had no idea this market existed, but once I saw the business for sale on eBay it seemed perfect. The seller explained he had purchased a new car with the money he had made with this business, and to someone that was totally broke and looking for a way to get out of the pile of bills under my butt, it sounded like a good idea.

What I did not know at the time was that the seller was affiliated with several other websites offering the identical service. Essentially I paid $1,100 for a template website that was being used by several other people. For all I knew the person that sold me the site under the impression he was getting out of the business, was in actuality operating under a new name, offering the same service of the business I had just purchased. One of those due diligence stories that makes you really wonder how strong the power of impulse must have been to make a stupid purchase like that one.

Not one to complain about this, since I did just buy a supposedly lucrative business for the bottom dollar price of $1,100, I decided to play around with the marketing of the business. Since the business aimed to serve forum owners that needed content on their website, I decided to try my hand at search engine marketing.

After signing up with Google AdWords pay-per-click marketing, I launched a keyword-based campaign that would show my advertisements when people searched terms on Google for forum posting services. Yes, people actually search those terms. I had no clue they did, but took a stab at it just in case. I figured if people were in fact searching Google for a forum posting service, then they would find my advertisement, sign up for my service, and money would be made. To my surprise, that is exactly what happened.

People would discover my business through my Google paid advertisements, and many of them would sign up for my service. Since I had virtually no money, I had to keep advertising cheap. Luckily Google AdWords operates on a bid per keyword basis. This means that the price that is paid every time someone clicks your ad on Google is actually determined by the amount bid on the term by you, and other businesses interested in advertising on that particular search term. Since this was a niche business to begin with, and since the conventional knowledge was that nobody searched terms like forum posting service, the bid per click was extremely low. I bid a maximum of 7 cents per click, and often ended up paying between 3 and 5 cents per click. This in turn meant I was receiving anywhere from 20 to 30 unique visitors per day to my website for the unbelievable cost of just $1 per day. In fact, my weekly cost for my entire advertising campaign was just $8. The business would sell a few hundred dollars in forum posting services, and this is how I made money.

The problems with the business were numerous. Getting people to post on forums for a few cents a post was often a challenge, as was finding people to post on forums with a wide variety of topics. In the end the business itself probably took more time than it was worth, but the concept remains viable to this day.

Back to the e-book. I had all but stopped posting on forums by early July, and was in the process of selling the business to another eBay member for, you guessed it, $1,100. I wasn't going to earn much on the sale of the business, but at least I was able to move on from it without losing too much. It was at this point that it struck me those Internet marketers at the Warrior Forum might be interested in knowing about the business, and how I was able to make hundreds of dollars of revenue with just $8 a week in advertising. After all I was in the process of selling it, so I had nothing to lose if every single reader decided to build their company to compete with it. Even the buyer seemed half interested at best of continuing the service.

That Friday night in early July I wrote about 17 pages, detailing my entire process of advertising this business on Google. While I was writing the book it occurred to me that this was information never before heard of. People were commonly paying Google upwards of $1 or more per click in many popular industries, leaving me to believe that this information would be very valuable to the right people.

I decided to charge $299 for my e-book, and offer it with the rights for distribution and resale. This is commonly known in the industry as private label rights. I figured there was not going to be a long life to this e-book, and I had nothing to lose by selling it for a lot of money, since it would limit the amount of buyers, and if I could just sell 1 or 2 my life would be infinitely better, at least for a few days.

At the time listing special offers on the Warrior Forum's special offer board was free of charge. It is now about $20 to do this same thing. After spending an hour writing the sales letter for this e-book, I posted my advertisement on the special offer board. It was late, I was tired and not sure if the book would sell at all.

Two days had passed and my offer had yet to be approved by the moderators of the forum. Finally, early in the morning of the third day after I had posted the offer it went live. Within minutes I had sold 5 copies, and received over a thousand dollars into my PayPal account. I couldn't believe what had happened, and the truth was this was just the beginning.

After answering dozens of questions, and spending nearly 48 hours straight on the computer monitoring my offer online, the totals were staggering. I had sold over twenty copies, made over $6,000, and had people emailing me asking for the sequel. It was in that moment that I realized the power of writing and selling an e-book that was in demand. There are no geographic borders or boundaries when you sell an e-book online. I had buyers from Germany, England, California and Indonesia. I had no company, no staff, no inventory and when I started no money, yet all of a sudden I had a global business.

Even though at the time my life was full of problems, I took my girlfriend to Hilton Head Island for the July 4th holiday weekend, staying in an ocean front hotel room for 3 nights. It was at this time I vividly remember thinking this is one of the greatest feelings in the world. I had gone from depressed and destitute to having enough money in the bank to take an impromptu vacation and eat at fine restaurants in just three days, the feeling was absolutely exhilarating.

I have since gone on to write over a dozen short e-books on a variety of topics, most of which have sold very well. However most of my e-book income comes from my ghostwriting service. My company ghostwrites between ten and fifteen e-books each month for a wide variety of clients. Looking back on it, I had a long way to go, a lot more bills needed to be paid off before I would take another trip like that, but the truth was, for at least one weekend I felt things were back to normal, in the most unusual sort of ways.

Whether you want to publish your own e-book, or ghostwrite for others, this chapter aims to give you a fair and accurate definition of the industry, and how you can profit from it.

Definition

An e-book is typed document, typically produced in a word processor that is sold as a downloadable file over the Internet. The document is often converted into PDF format for easy readability and security against fraud.

E-books come in all shapes and sizes. Some e-books are delivered as HTML files, while others are delivered in popular DOC format. Some e-books have cover and interior graphics, while others remain entirely text-based.

E-books are sold for costs ranging from $.01 to $5,000, and are often priced high enough to provide a commission to marketers that are known as affiliates. Some e-books are given away for free as promotional items by businesses as diverse as online auto dealerships to plastic surgeons.

E-books do not require a license to distribute, nor do they require a barcode or ISBN number like their printed brethren often do.

MODES OF ACQUISITION

Coming across e-book related work is not hard to do. The majority of freelance writing job boards such as Guru.com and Elance.com offer a variety of e-book writing jobs for bid. Further, one can produce an e-book for one's own purposes to sell by simply identifying a hungry market that needs help solving a problem, and then writing an e-book that delivers an answer to the problem.

When it comes to freelance writing, getting the gig as an e-book writer often depends on a number of factors including price per page or per word, the portfolio or sample e-books the writer has to show the client and the time frame in which the writer can produce the e-book.

Those determined to write e-books will have little resistance, since one simply needs a computer and a word processing program such as MS WORD or the free Open Office to produce e-books. If you need it, you can pick up a free copy of Open Office by visiting www.OpenOffice.Org.

WHAT TO EXPECT IN TERMS OF PAY

E-books surprisingly have a fairly regular market rate per page for writers to adhere to. The rate varies between $8 and $30 per page, however most of my company's clients pay a flat rate of $10 per page. This rate seems to be competitive, even somewhat low, and positions the writer to obtain the optimal amount of work. For those that are interested in charging a larger rate there is hope. Some well known e-book writers charge as much as $30 per page for their work, and seem to stay busy producing content for those clients that want exceptional content.

One writer that has been successful in charging a premium per page amount for e-book projects is Tiffany Dow. You can check out her blog by visiting www.TiffanyDow.com/Blog.

Producing e-books also involves doing menial organizational tasks such as setting the table of contents to hyperlink to each page, adding citations and source information, and in some cases inserting royalty free images into the book when appropriate. It is understood by most experienced e-book buyers that these services will require a separate fee based entirely on the time it takes to perform these tasks.

It is recommended that if you are ghostwriting e-books for clients, it makes sense to partner with a graphic designer familiar with making e-book related graphics, also known as e-covers. Knowing a talented graphic designer can secure a new source of income for your writing business through referral commissions. Essentially when a client orders an e-book, they will ask you for references of a good graphic designer to create a cover for the e-book. In some cases, the client will in fact ask you create e-book graphics. In either case it is highly recommended that you refer these clients to your preferred graphic designer in trade for an affiliate commission from the designer. Just telling your clients to let the designer know you sent them is usually enough. Of course, a special website link can be passed on to your client to ensure you receive a commission for the client's e-book graphic package order. Some enjoy just passing on business to fellow freelancers, while others, like myself, work the cost of graphics into full package e-books in order to receive a commission on the sales of graphics. Since graphic work is similar to writing in the way that the only upfront cost of production is time, prices can be negotiated based on the promise of future business. I have several graphic artist partners that have literally produced over 50 sets of e-cover graphics for me in the past year. Whatever lower price they have given my company was worth it in the sheer volume of new business I have sent their way.

Tips for Getting the Job Done Quickly and Efficiently

Once hired to produce an e-book, the time quickly arrives to actually write the thing. While there are many different ways to write an e-book, I find one method particularly effective. Free writing, the art of writing without editing, can be a writer's best friend when producing e-books for clients.

Free writing allows the writer to produce a larger amount of content in a shorter period of time. This method is imperative to writing e-books when the per page rate pay is in the $10 or below range. It will likely take a substantial amount of pages to earn a sizeable income. Thus, the free writing technique can be the engine that drives your business into the profitable lane. Free writing often works best when it is related to a topic you are already familiar with. An example could be the pet store worker writing an e-book about the cost and maintenance of a fish tank. Since the pet store staff member already works with these tanks on a regular basis, writing an e-book on the topic can be done almost entirely off the knowledge that already exists in their head. Of course some facts will need to be researched online, but none should take more than a few minutes of doing a Google search, and reviewing reliable websites.

The beauty of most e-books is that their topics are often based on how to fix a common problem. The how-to genre of e-books is so prevalent eBay has dedicated an entire category of its online marketplace to it, where most of the e-books sold on eBay are to this day located. Writing how-to e-books often takes a few references, some common sense, and a simple outline to complete.

As with most writing assignments, those that organize an assignment prior to beginning the writing process will be better off. While there are some caveats to this method, like getting so bogged down in research your writing takes days to start, for the most part the organize first then free write. This seems to work best for completing e-books.

After completing the e-book, a general read-through and an edit will be necessary. Once the e-book has been cleaned up, it is time to send the finished draft to the client for approval. Typically this is done via email by simply sending the e-book file as an attachment in an email message.

Disadvantages

The two major disadvantages of writing an e-book is the time it takes to complete and getting paid by the client. The time it takes to complete an e-book can be staggering. If you are commissioned to write a 100 page e-book, or God forbid, a 200 page e-book those single spaced pages could take years to complete. It is for this reason I recommend only accepting projects of 50 pages or less to start. Listen to my audio recordings for more rationale on why it is important to start with a manageable size, and how most e-books shouldn't be more than 25 pages long.

The payment issue can also be a major pitfall of writing e-books for clients as a ghostwriter. The type of person that wants an e-book done is often the same type of person that has yet to budget enough money to pay for the project. If you leave any money to be paid after completion expect a wait, in many cases, expect a long wait.

To fight the common problem of late payments by clients, simply require full payment upfront in advance of writing anything. I do this for almost all our e-book projects, and while at first people did drag their feet a bit, within a few weeks of requiring funds most clients simply pay. They get to know you, realize you are going to honor the commitment and complete the e-book to its fullest, so they will pay in advance if you continue to require it to be that way.

Future Opportunities

The future of e-books is in multimedia. Since the first day I logged into the Warrior Forum to discuss Internet marketing I realized the huge, and apparently immediately impending replacement of the e-book with audio and video. While that time has yet to arrive, global surveys have shown that large percentages of people online watch video every single day, leading most to believe the e-book will at some point become a blend of video, audio, and of course text.

For now e-books are as strong as they ever have been. With Amazon's release of the Kindle, an easy to use e-book reader that took years for their team of tech wizards to develop, you can rest assured e-books will be around for a long time to come. With the advanced exposure of e-books to regular everyday people the past stigma of e-books as being nothing more than digital scam letters is also dissolving. Even among my own family and friends, the fact that I work in the e-book industry is no longer looked at as a pyramid scheme. Instead, it is now looked at with only modest skepticism, which means e-books have come a long way!

Market Domination Capacity

At the time of publication not one marketer has put together a full package e-book ghostwriting service that includes a sales letter, cover graphics, and a compelling custom e-book. I have been fiddling with this concept for years, but have yet to nail it. My first monetary success online in the service business was a site called Marketer Bank, you can check out a no longer in use variation of it at www.MarketerBank.com. In terms of market domination, one can absolutely become the go-to provider for e-book creation. There are hundreds, if not thousands of people that provide this service on a case by case basis, but no provider to date has been able to capture a large market share, despite this author's best efforts. So the chances are good to dominate this market, and the chances to capture a segment or niche of this market is absolutely incredible.

Chapter 3
SEO Article Writing

Back when I was still crazy enough to think being an adjunct professor of speech communications would pay my bills, I would read the Wall Street Journal each morning before class. Reading the paper gave me a sense of fulfillment from a world I had recently left.

Working in apparel was one of the more gratifying jobs I had ever had. People choosing you as a fashion expert over nearly anyone else in your city, getting written up in the paper for trend setting designs, and meeting unique and often eccentric yet creative individuals was just part of the allure of working in fashion. When the small boutique I had opened two years earlier closed, a part of me shut off as well.

In the spirit of keeping the mind fresh, and not letting my business savvy go to waste, I kept my two hundred dollar a year subscription to the Wall Street Journal, justifying it as a necessary expense in figuring out what was going on in the business world, and how I could one day make a comeback. I was the only person on my low income neighborhood's block to receive this paper. In fact, I was the only person on the block to receive any newspaper each day!

Taking the Wall Street Journal to class each day also helped me avoid the pre-class chit-chat offered by those students that arrived as early as I did. I enjoyed talking with students to an extent, but I preferred to keep things professional and deliver the bulk of my words during class time. At the time I was teaching 5 public speaking classes at the University of South Carolina. In college teaching terms, that is a year's worth of teaching in one semester. Little did I know I would read an article that would contribute to a business that nets over six figures a year in profit and is continually growing larger and larger by the day. The same business that has empowered over 300 people to become part time freelance writers and do everything from buy groceries to get that new HD flat screen TV they've always wanted. All from a little company I started after reading one article.

One morning I sat in my classroom at the University of South Carolina where I was teaching, hunched over the teacher's desk at the front of the class flipping through the Marketplace section of the Wall Street Journal. An article caught my eye about online writing being a labor for the poorest of poor writers.

As I started to read the article I realized quickly it was all about SEO articles. The same article jobs I had seen on the online freelance job boards such as Elance.com and Guru.com up for bid like wildfire. The writer had cleverly disguised herself as a freelance writer and bid on some of these SEO article projects. She wrote about her experience, how the client actually requested her not to include certain facts about the topic she was writing on, and how at the end of the day the pay was so miserable no sane writer would want to do these jobs. The article really focused on the lack of quality and at the same time unbelievably low pay for these search engine friendly articles. This writer of course was at the pinnacle of her writing career, as a feature writer for the Wall Street Journal, one of the largest newspapers in the world. What did she know about what people would be willing to accept for their writing, I remember thinking.

As I finished reading the article it became apparent to me that people are in need of these articles at an alarming rate, and me being a totally broke teacher, getting paid dismally for my work didn't seem all that bad. I made a note to start researching this type of work as soon as I returned from classes that day.

Coming to the understanding of a market void was a major epiphany for me. At the time there was no large writing firm based out of America that was sucking it up and writing for a few dollars a page. For me, all other avenues I had researched about making money were much harder than it was to sit down for 3 hours and write 10 articles on a random topic. I was fortunate enough to charge $8 or so per page when I started out. This gave me enough money to buy food, pay some bills, and continue to research this seemingly insatiable demand for SEO articles.

Now I know what you are most likely thinking, I want to be a freelance writer, not a robot that makes less than minimum wage to write meaningless garbage. My answer to this is simple. I have not written one of those articles in a year, and yet I still make the majority of my monthly income from SEO articles. So, before you toss the computer out the window and swear never to charge less than $100 a page, take a breath and realize in this circumstance low wages are a good thing.

After spending some months writing these SEO articles I figured out two important conclusions. The first is that people were willing to settle for articles that were fairly basic. Such as a who, what, when, where, why theme type article. Secondly, I noticed the demand for SEO articles was, and still is, insatiable.

The absolute unending demand for fresh custom SEO articles is due to one reason, the search engines. Search engines such as Google reward fresh content on websites with higher placement in their results. What does that matter you might wonder? The answer is simple, the higher a website places in the natural results, the more money the website will be able to make without advertising.

SEO articles are in fact the means by which most companies attempt to have their website rank in the search engines. The articles are used to both populate a website and submit to directories that create high value links for the submitter. In the end all you really need to know is that these little one page 500 word articles are gold for people that want to place high in the search engines. You can check out a popular directory where people submit SEO articles, and get a chance to read through some of these little pieces of gold at www.EzineArticles.com.

Placing high in the search engines for many businesses is a matter of profit and loss. Advertising online can be expensive and sometimes unrewarding. In order to truly maximize the potential of a website one needs to receive free targeted traffic, which almost always comes from search engines like Google.

The important fact here is that search engine optimization articles are red hot, and as long as you are willing to swallow your pride and take a smaller per page rate than most freelance writers would, the demand is insatiable.

From doing my own work and reading the article in the Wall Street Journal it became apparent to me that where most people do not want to go is often the best place to find an opportunity to make money.

Definition

SEO articles are typically 1 page articles on a given keyword phrase that range from 300 to 600 words in length. These articles are often produced in sets of 10, 20, 30, 50, and 100 article batches.

SEO articles are typically based on simple explanations of a keyword phrase. The article typically mentions the designated keyword phrase approximately 3 to 5% of the time. If an article is 500 words, the keyword phrase would be repeated anywhere from 10 to 25 times throughout the article. Most SEO articles are logically written with an introduction two to three body paragraphs and a conclusion.

While some articles call for special arrangements, most SEO articles do not include links, and remain unbiased to any given subject. They are often more of a description of something than a sales piece of persuasive article.

Modes of Acquisition

SEO article jobs are virtually everywhere on the net. Since there are no major firms that cover all the needs of the website and search engine optimizers, finding this type of work is fairly easy.

SEO article jobs are often listed on freelance boards such as Elance.com and Guru.com, as well as secondary boards such as RentACoder.com and Scriptlance.com.

I have found that after several months of writing on your own customer referrals alone will account for a large part of your writing business. For every 10 customers my company services today at least 3 of them came as referrals from other customers.

Easy to navigate websites are a great way to offer SEO writing services. You can check mine out at www.GuestProfessor.com it has changed very little since being built two years ago. Most websites that offer SEO article writing services are poorly constructed for those interested in making a purchase. Be sure to offer easy ways for users to buy the service right away, and several samples for users to review on your website for higher conversion rates.

What to Expect in Terms of Pay

The going rate for SEO style articles is around $7 to $10 per page. Some writers, and SEO firms charge as much as $30 per page, while other freelancers will charge as little as $2 per page. The average is around $6 for non-U.S. writers and around $8 for U.S. writers per page. A page is defined as a single spaced document 500 or so words in length.

Typically SEO articles are sold in batches, such as a batch of 10 articles would go for $100 if you were to charge $10 per page.

I own a content creation firm that is strictly stocked with U.S. writers, whom produce content for less than $5 per page. They are not professional copywriters, nor do they aspire to be, many of the writers on my staff are stay at home moms, graduate students, real estate agents, teachers, etc., all interested in earning extra cash.

Building this team was not easy, and I do not recommend it to anyone that is not serious about spending time training and managing the writers. However, in the process it has been shown that people will write for several dollars a page if they are paid quickly, paid on time and given very simple assignments to do. In return the writers do not have to deal with issues clients often levy on providers like complaining, update requests, bartering, nonpayment, etc. In short, the writers on my team don't make that much money per page, but assume very little risk, no marketing expense and are paid on time regardless of whether the end client pays me for the work or not.

While we have had some clients that have literally stolen thousands of dollars worth of articles from us without paying, for the most part this relationship is lucrative. On occasion the writers will think that I portray my company as a one man show, but in reality, most of my websites explicitly explain that we have a large team of writers, and when we deliver 100 articles in 2 days time, does the client really believe I wrote every one of them myself? Further, team-building and maintaining can be difficult because staff members rarely take the time to understand how much a customer costs to acquire. Our marketing expenses range in the several hundred to several thousand dollar range per week, making the seemingly lucrative relationship at times a razor thin profit margin game. At other times it goes up. In the end, it's a business that seems to function well enough.

My team has allowed me to write very little when it comes to SEO articles, and keep the billing at just $10 or so per article. This allows for the writers to be paid, my administrative staff to be paid, the monthly software, advertising and hosting fees to be paid, and a modest profit to be made as well.

The reason I explain my process is to help you understand no matter where your writing is, or what you think your per page rate should be, the way to make SEO article production work is to look for methods to keep competitive on price, and creatively get the content produced.

Going into business producing SEO articles for a high ticket price is possible, but ironically much more difficult. I have personally written SEO articles for a major billion dollar company that is a national advertiser, top traffic getter, and all around supersized web business. They have been around since the early days of the web, and if I told you their company name chances are you have heard of them. For this special project, since the client was such a big name, I choose to write the articles myself rather than giving the work to my team. I was paid $50 per article, went through about 3 rewrites per article, and had to wait 6 weeks to get paid. I also had to deal with several managers, an accounting issue, and a grump copywriter that was seemingly asking for things to be fixed because she had nothing else to do, isn't that what all writers think of editors? Either way, working for the big time company was not only not a great job, it sucked.

Since I wrote those articles myself, the overhead was nothing, and the profit was around $500. The time it took for me to produce, revise, and beg for payment was approximately 13 hours. While some might still think this is a worthwhile venture, I challenge you to do the assignment yourself and see if it is really that lucrative. Further, finding one of these clients was literally 1 in 1,000. Since I have worked with over 1,000 companies, webmasters, people, small business owners, and so forth, this was the only time I have ever charged more than $20 for an SEO article, I can tell you it is not an easy client to come by. Thus, it does not make sense to try to charge a big chunk of change for SEO article content, even the sassy Wall Street Journal writer came to that conclusion at the end of that wonderful article I keep mentioning.

Taking the figure of $500 for 13 hours of work, let us compare that to selling 100 articles at $10 per article to a typical one person website owner. This order would bring in $1,000 in revenue, and after paying the writers, and paying merchant fees, you would net around $500 profit. The time to dispatch these 100 articles would be about 30 minutes if you had a nice network of writers available, and the time to sort and deliver them would be about 1 hour. So, the total time invested in this project would be less than 2 hours, and the profit would be the same, and in turn you are not paying other writers to do work, which builds your network of loyal service providers. In short, everyone wins.

The above is an over-simplified example. Often clients that want larger groups of content will ask for a price break, some orders can get as low as $5 or $6 per article, which means your profit will be much less. The difference is that people will typically need more articles in the future, and thus your volume will increase.

So instead of immediately trying to bill a large sum of money, think of creative ways like the one above to keep rates in line with what others are charging and still come out ahead of the pack in terms of profit.

Tips for Getting the Job Done Quickly and Efficiently

SEO articles, whether you write them, or have others write them for you, all need to be done in a similar fashion. People are paying for these articles because they want natural flowing text with keywords included to trigger the search engine links. This means you want to keep the articles clear, to the point and offer keyword optimization by including the keyword phrase at least a few times in each paragraph.

Many writers will believe it makes sense to just jumble these articles up because nobody will read them. This is a mistake, not only will the clients read these articles, but search engine spiders that review the content are becoming more savvy, and thus more aware of poorly constructed content.

Therefore the key to getting SEO articles done is making sure they are original with no previously published content in them, as well as making sure they are optimized for the keyword phrase, and make sense to the end reader.

Disadvantages

The biggest disadvantage in the world of SEO article creation is plagiarism. The temptation of searching online for relevant information and pasting it into the article is just too great for many writers to resist. Combine this temptation with low pay, and often demanding clients and a recipe for disaster emerges. Be disciplined, and realize the client wants 100% original content coming from your brain to the keyboard directly. Make each article original, and you should be in great shape.

Future Opportunities

SEO articles will be around for a longtime to come. As long as the search engines place a high value on relative original content, and relevant links, SEO articles will be the primary mode of getting there. The people that produce SEO articles on a regular and timely basis can expect business to be robust for a longtime to come.

Further, as long as there are affordable methods to getting content produced, you will find even the smallest of websites looking for original content. Therefore it is evident that SEO articles as an online content source will be red hot for a longtime to come.

MARKET DOMINATION CAPACITY

Market domination for producing SEO articles is possible but not likely. Since so many webmasters find themselves in need of unique content it is very hard to capture an entire market. Trust me, I have tried. The other problem with total market domination is the fact that most webmasters have unique and specific needs. For example, a webmaster that owns a discussion forum on college athletics, might want to order 20 profiles of college teams from across the country. This requires specific research, formatting, etc. While another client is a realtor from Charlotte, North Carolina, that wants content related to their area of which they hope to sell houses in. This requires a different kind of research, and requires a different kind of article, more acute to what the realtor could use on his or her blog.

Therefore it is possible, but challenging to dominate the market of SEO content. Getting into a niche, and dominating it is much easier. Last time I checked there were no expert SEO content creators for the mortgage business, nor were there any for the bakery business, and so on. Becoming an expert in a niche can help your business boom in this industry.

Chapter 4
Sales Letter Writing

Writing sales letters is an art that started over a hundred years ago with the advent of mail order catalogs and direct mail campaigns. As long as the post office in some form or another has been around, so has the sales letter. Sales copy, (or sales letters as they are commonly referred to on the Internet), play a great role in the Internet marketers' toolkit. While the web 2.0 movement is helping to curb the long form sales letter from its position of sales inducing prosperity, it is still a viable way for Internet marketers to make money. The problem with most Internet marketers, and others that attempt to make money online, is that they do not have the writing skills to properly communicate their sales message in a long form sales letter. Thus, a market emerges for writers with a flare for the sensational, dramatic, emotion-induced writing that good sales letters demand.

Dating, love advice, how to attract women, are just some of the topics I do not know that much about. I've been dating the same wonderful woman for four years. Before her I was somewhat clumsy when it came to meeting the opposite sex. I'd talk to almost anyone, and kind of wait to see what they thought of me. I was not exactly a dating or attraction wizard. It was therefore somewhat remarkable to me that I was being paid $350 for a 5 page sales letter selling an e-book on how to attract women like honey does bees. The other surprise of being offered this job was that I had never formally been paid to write a sales letter up to that point in my online freelance writing career.

How can one person with seemingly no relevance to the topic, and no experience in performing the job at hand, get hired for a relatively high fee? The answer is that nobody really does affordable long form sales letters anymore. Instead, the perceived value of a good sales letter that converts prospects and leads into buyers is so high, that those few people that consider themselves sales copy experts, charge thousands of dollars per page.

My perspective when it comes to freelance writing has always been based on a simple formula. Find out what the other people are charging, and then charge about 20 to 50 percent less than the competition. This formula seems to work extremely well for newbie writers, as it did for me. Whether people like to admit it or not, many potential buyers base a good portion of their hiring decision on the cost of services provided. Even if your skills are not as good, and your experience is not as great as the completion, if your price is low enough, a buyer will most of the time seriously consider hiring you.

Why is this fact true, why does the price trump all theory work well on the Internet? The answer is in the question, the Internet is a new medium for buyers, where people like you and me, not big corporations with millions of dollars, are the buyers. Therefore, the buyers are typically strapped for cash, and are looking for a way to build a website that will possibly make money, and most importantly not spend a fortune in the process.

Think about it, how many successful Internet businesses boast about how little money and time they invested in their brilliant idea? Most of the them unfortunately do, and this attitude of spend less get more trickles down to those businesses looking to maintain a relationship with a freelance writer to help write their sales copy. The spirit of the Internet has always been based around this concept of making affordability a marquee aspect of any given situation online. Think about how search giant Google allows people to market online, by opening every search term up for unbiased bid. Think about their IPO, and the auction format that attempted to do the same. In a world where millions can be made faster than ever, the online user is taught spending less, or better yet, nothing is the way to go.

Many think this theory of the low price bid winning most of the time only applies to small rookie clients, the truth is the opposite is true. The theory mainly applies to established Internet marketers and those online looking for writing services, as they are the ones that know that using the Internet is a way to get things done cheaply.

I personally wrote for more Internet millionaires in my first year than I have ever since. In fact one of my very first clients paid me very little to do over twenty pages of training materials. Since he was using his real name, and since I was writing his company's training materials, it did not take much effort to find out this gentleman was making a fortune on the Internet selling a $2,000 online education course. Today I could literally point you to a video of him online talking about his net worth being in the tens of millions of dollars. He paid approximately ten bucks a page for material he was selling for twenty times as much.

Conversely, new Internet marketers and webmasters are more susceptible to paying high dollar amounts for sales copy as they think it is the norm. The lack of experience, or knowledge of so-called going rates for online freelance jobs leaves people susceptible to paying what one might pay a copywriter for an offline job. If you want to work for those successful in online marketing, be prepared to have your slice of the humble rate pie.

Regardless of the experience of the client, the bottom line is sales letters and sales copy written for a website are typically regarded as a high dollar service. Those that are established copywriters charge around $3,000 to $20,000 for a typical 10 to 20 page job. Obviously most people cannot afford to pay that rate, so where do they turn? Most likely the people either write the copy themselves, or try to find a discount provider, which is difficult since most people feel compelled to charge a large sum of money for what is really not a difficult task.

Back to the dating e-book mentioned earlier in this chapter. As I was marketing a different product online, someone noticed my sales letter, and asked if I could do one for them. I agreed, and charged them $350, and wrote my butt off for a day about dating and attracting the woman of your dreams.

After a few revisions I was paid promptly, and have not heard from the client since. It is this type of experience that should lead you to seriously consider becoming a sales letter writer. It is not only lucrative, it is a wide open field, since most sales copy writers are simply put way overpriced for the average Joe that needs the service done, the market is ripe for a provider that offers the quality of craft that a seasoned professional does with a lower, more affordable rate.

DEFINITION

Sales copy or a sales letter as it is commonly referred to, is a long form piece of writing often posted on a website that serves as the replacement for a salesperson. The letter typically describes the product in detail, attempts to connect with the reader through emotional and psychological mechanisms such as fear of loss, deep understanding, prompting a sense of urgency, or making the reader understand why their life would be drastically improved if they purchased the product or service being pitched in the letter.

Sales letters vary in length, but tend to be fairly long winded. They can run anywhere from 3 pages all the way up to over 100 pages. The typical sales letter online is around 20 to 30 pages long, and contains extra items such as buyer or user testimonials, bonus descriptions, bullet points, audio, video, pictures, charts, illustrations, product images, and some type of money back guarantee.

Sales copy and sales letters are often produced in an effort to gain new prospects through the lead generation process of giving away a free report, item, or piece of valuable information in exchange for a name, address, email address, and so on. Sales letters are also used to sell a product or service through a website. They are often integrated with an email newsletter subscription name and address boxes, as well as merchant account checkout buttons such as the ones offered by PayPal, Google Checkout and other merchant service providers.

MODES OF ACQUISITION

Obtaining new business when it comes to sales letters often depends on personal relationships, and client referrals. Since the high dollar writers typically dominate the pay per click advertising space on search engines, it is often a wise move to market your services to online marketing forums, and through online classified ads.

While one does not need a website to gain new business, it is common to have a website to both offer samples of previous sales letters written, and to offer a mode by which the customer can purchase the service. Websites also are good for offering background on a writer's particular expertise, and what the sales letter writing process involves when it comes to the client.

Another popular way to gain sales letter writing business is by bidding on relevant projects on the major freelance boards such as Elance.com and Guru.com. While these boards have a number of sales letter writing assignments posted for open bid at any given time, it is best to bid with a website link to offer the client a quick review of the samples you have produced for this genre of writing.

Finally, sales copy jobs can easily be gained from offline clients through direct mail, post cards, cold calling, and walking door-to-door discussing your service with local businesses. Typically local businesses are not yet schooled on the power of direct marketing, which of course is the root and birth of this style of writing, and thus you can educate the potential client while attracting new business at the same time.

What to Expect in Terms of Pay

Out of all the online writing methods to profit listed in this book, no method has a more diverse going rate or fee than sales letter writing. The bottom line is that most copywriters charge large sums of money, making the average going rate much higher than it should be. In my experience charging a client $100 per page for sale letters of 5 or more pages is appropriate. I believe with the right skills, and proper samples one could charge upwards of $300 per page.

Sales letter writing rates are the most ambiguous and least proven in the entire book since the market is so large, and so diverse in terms of actual fees being paid. One should absolutely use caution when providing a quote to a potential client that the quote is not too high. It is often best to ask the client what the project budget is, and see if you can somehow agree to an amicable price for all involved. If the client has done any research on the fees of copywriting and long form sales letters, chances are your bid will be low and affordable in their estimation compared to other comparable providers.

Tips for Getting the Job Done Quickly and Efficiently

Producing sales letters is ultimately a matter of research and focus. Since you are in essence writing a letter that acts as a replacement for a real life salesmen, it is first important to understand what you are trying to sell. The better you know the product, the more persuasive your sales letter will be.

Next, it is important to identify the triggers that often are used in this genre of writing. If you are writing a sales letter about a diet supplement for example, it would be appropriate to look at some of the top selling diet supplement websites, and see what emotional triggers are used in the sales letters to get the reader to take action. Does the sales letter address social and cultural repercussions for being overweight? If so, then would it make sense for you to devote a portion of the sales letter you are writing to this same topic?

By no means am I advocating for copying, or even borrowing any direct information from others. Instead, I am asking you to simply review other relevant work that has been proven successful to get an idea of what emotional triggers are being used, and what you can put into your letter that might help the client sell more products.

Another benefit of reviewing similar product website sales letters in your niche is to understand the cadence used in the writing. What is the rhythm of the top 5 sales letters in your niche? How does each sales letter start, progress and end? Is it with short paragraphs, longer paragraphs, headlines, sub headlines or just one long narrative? The answer to these questions will help to shape your sales letter into a format that will be at least somewhat familiar to the client, as well as the prospects that end up reading it. In this business, parity is not such a bad thing.

Once your research has been done, it is time to write out an outline of the sales letter. I find by creating a sales letter that is organized in some fashion before the writing begins you can include all the pertinent information in a well thought out process. Once writing sales letters becomes a daily task for you, the need for an outline may dwindle, but for those just getting started it is imperative to keep organized and look at the big picture. Many new copywriters will start out freestyle writing only to realize after a page and a half all their ideas have been put on paper. This occurrence can be stifling. In order to avoid it, proper organization and a big picture review needs to take place prior to the writing of the sales letter itself.

Once the organization is set in place, the writing can begin. Remember to keep the writing personal, emotional and sensational. This is not a time to be modest about the product you are attempting to sell. Nor is it a time to hold back, and be objective about what you are trying to get the reader to do.

You must not only demand the reader to take action, you must present the absolute reasons why it is imperative to take action today. Web traffic is incredibly fickle, and most that hire sales letter writers are simply looking to make their site as sticky as possible. This means that people go to the site, stay on the site, and end up buying something. Asking the prospect to think about something will do nothing more than waste everyone's time. Instead, be clear, be sensational, be over the top, be persuasive.

If you are able to master this process business will not only increase for your freelance writing operation, it will also increase for any venture you put online, since the key to selling almost anything online is persuasive writing.

Now that the outline and draft of the sales letter is done, it is important to look at the entire project from a distance, literally. Open a new document in your word processor, and zoom out to 30% of the original page view. This will open up enough space for you to see a broad picture of what your first five or six pages will look like to the reader that chooses to just skim the letter. Write out some type of cue or idea for several sections on each page. Little notes are fine for this step, you can even change the font to a different color, so you will remember to delete your notes before passing the draft on to the client.

After you have made some notes about how to make the sales letter more effective, add in sub headlines for every twist or turn in your story. Doing this is very similar to the writer or layout professional at a magazine that pulls several of the best quotes in the article and makes them large bolded out parts of the page to give readers a quick glance at what the article is all about. Creating eye-catching sub headlines can literally be a life saver for those that choose not to read the entire sales letter word for word.

Disadvantages

The biggest pitfall to sales letter writing is thinking you can do it without actually trying. I have had many a junior writer try their hand at sales copy and fail miserably. In fact, one of my company's many custom products is a 25 page e-book on a topic chosen by the client accompanied with a 5 page sales letter. Without going into too much detail, the sales letter is constantly the point of contention with the client when we finish the work. The junior writers are using a prebuilt template that gives them all the cues they need, and they are 100% of the time the original authors of the 25 page e-book that we are trying to sell, yet still they manage to write less than acceptable sales letters.

Why is it so hard to write a letter that sells? I am not sure of the reason specifically, but I think it often has to do with a tendency for writers to be underwhelmed with the product they are trying to write a sales letter for. I think that the best sales letters come from people believe in what they are writing about.

Personally I do not write sales copy for many people anymore. I might do 2 or 3 sales letters a year, and they are often for friends or old clients that I decide would be a good fit for my writing style. The main reason I don't take more sales letter related work is that I find myself only really invested deeply in my own projects enough to write sales copy for them. The sales copy usually works pretty well, at least good enough to sell whatever I am doing at the moment, and thus I stick with focusing my sales letter writing on my own marketing efforts. Thus, it is important to realize unless you truly share a passion for your client's product or service, it will be difficult to write a compelling sales letter for them.

This pitfall should not deter you from writing sales letters. I have a privileged existence as a writer that can choose what projects to do, and which ones to pass on. Two years ago I was not in the same situation, and would have gladly written about chipmunks, shipwrecks, soy milk or any other topic that I have no interest or direct knowledge in for the few hundred bucks in profit. The reason I would have taken those jobs is that I know with enough research, and enough forward thinking I could develop a passion for the topic strong enough to write something powerful for people to read. If you are just getting started, realize that for the right amount of cash it is pretty easy to get highly enthused about a particular subject. Sounds callous I know, but I think most would agree with the statement regardless. Sales letter writing is all about passion, and often money and the approval of others can be used as a great motivator to find a passionate approach to nearly any topic.

FUTURE OPPORTUNITIES

Sales letters are quickly becoming a thing of the past due to the advent of video and audio streaming technology online. There are still plenty of people looking for sales letter writers, but I predict this will change as the Internet becomes a greater part of people's lives. Long form sales letters take a long time to read, and often are congested with meaningless stories and scripted testimonials. It is thus my opinion that for now the market is very much open for new writers, but those writers may want to consider this a supplemental income rather than putting all their eggs into this one basket.

MARKET DOMINATION CAPACITY

The chances of market domination are extremely good for those that want to charge a reasonable rate and bill themselves as the affordable alternative. The Internet is full of egotistical overpriced copywriters that bill themselves out of most of the business online. The Internet is also filled with talented copywriters that do not have a clue about how to brand themselves, make a compelling website, and market with the correct search engines online. It is therefore wide open for domination under the above circumstance. It is also open to dominate if you were to gather a team of writers, and sell a service that provided a fast turnaround on template style sales letters that are customized for each client's specific needs.

Chapter 5
Press Release Writing

Just over a year ago, in the back of a 15 passenger van coming home from Memphis, I first realized press releases were a lucrative form of freelance writing. At the time I was working on a project for a seasoned publicity specialist, that had somehow found one of my websites, and offered me a few writing gigs to do his overflow of press release jobs, as well as create a sales page for his website.

Since the drive from Memphis, Tennessee to my home in Columbia, South Carolina is of the all day variety, and since I was in the back row of this van, with little space to spread out and sleep, I decided to whip out the laptop and do some work for my client, the publicity specialist. As the work got done, I realized if this person was in fact as busy as I thought he was, and if he was in fact telling me the truth about what his clients thought of my writing, and how much they enjoyed reading my press releases, than I might as well consider making a small business out of this popular form of business writing.

What in the world was I doing in the back of a passenger van you might be wondering? Coming home from a trip with friends where we saw a bowl game between the University of Houston and my graduate school Alma matter the University of South Carolina Gamecocks. It's funny how trips, and time off in general can tweak the mind just enough to realize seemingly obvious things such as new business opportunities staring you right in the face. If I had stayed in my world of daily writing, coffee drinking, and of course, Internet marketing without coming up for air, I am not sure this opportunity to write press releases would have come to light.

It has been 1 year since I took that trip, and my press release writing business is the second largest operation I own and operate at this time. I have written hundreds of press releases in the past year, and have worked with over 200 PR clients. I have tested and tracked hundreds press release campaigns, and worked tirelessly to become the chosen provider for those searching the Internet for a press release writer.

Several years prior to my Memphis trip I was living with a political consultant that wrote press releases daily. His goal was to announce everything the candidate was doing on a given day with a press release, and then email it to local media hoping it would get picked up. At the time I found press release writing to be worthless. Something people just ignored. The writing was bland, the message often insignificant, and to read one was almost as bad as picking up a DVD operation manual that people get when they buy a DVD player. In short, my first impression of reading and writing press releases was a bad one.

Luckily, the publicity specialist was able to help me see a different side of these 1 page announcements. He explained how they can help businesses gain valuable attention, and how when done correctly, can absolutely transform a business.

I took this message to heart, and when I started developing press releases, I wanted them to read like a story from a top tier newspaper. I wanted the media to pick them up, read the headline, and not be able to put the release down until the entire page was read.

I started small, creating a freely hosted blog, like those found on www.Blogger.com that I used as a website. I then promoted this tiny impromptu site I build in a day that sold custom press releases for $50 on the search engines, and got a small bit of business. Nearly all my customers told me the price I was charging was too small. In just two short weeks of launching my site things were looking good for my newest writing venture, the most affordable PR firm on the net.

Somewhere around the tenth or fifteenth press release I had written it hit me that there is a serious demand for this type of service. It was at this point I ratcheted up some money, invested in a real website to be built, and started marketing this service to the masses.

Within twenty minutes of launching my new website with a search engine marketing campaign I had already received an inquiry. Within hours I had my first order from the new site, and that is when I knew this was a business that would bear fruit for a longtime to come.

Today I receive orders for anywhere from 1 and 5 press releases per day, and have a hearty PR distribution business as well. You can check out my press release website at www.CustomPressRelease.com. The site went through probably 30 different variations before I settled on the current setup. Further, my advertising campaigns have often become too costly to continue, which has caused me to often lose money on this business when my advertising costs outweigh the amount of revenue being brought in. Building a freelance writing business site that offers PR services that converts into regular sales is not easy by any means, but the end product does tend to offer a simple solution to a potential clients problem.

There are plenty of negatives about doing press releases, mainly that clients are paying a lot of money for 1 page, and thus they expect it to be perfect, and mesh exactly with their vision. Also nearly every client that hires you to write a press release for them will expect some type of affordable distribution offer. Unfortunately the way the premier newswires are setup, press release distribution is a relatively expensive thing to do.

Looking back one year in hindsight I realize that creating and nurturing the press release writing service has been by far one of the best choices I have made in my business career. The potential for publicity services is enormous and I greatly urge anyone that reads this book to give some serious thought about getting into the business in some fashion or another. While the negatives mentioned above are serious enough to deter some away from trying their hand at this business at all, there are great rewards waiting for those that dare to overcome these obstacles with creative thinking and grassroots online marketing.

Definition

A press release is a newsworthy announcement typically 1 page in length, most likely 400 words or less, that offers an attributable headline accompanied by a body of text that delivers details on the announcement. Press releases are often used to gain media attention, deliver important company information, and offer compliance to financial markets through formatted company announcements such as quarterly earnings statements.

A press release can be sent out alone, or included in a larger media kit. A good press release can serve as a vital way to obtain media attention without spending money on advertising. Press releases are also often used to gain link relevance in the search engines through online distribution channels. Most press release distribution companies offer an online component that when utilized will build hundreds, if not thousands, of unique links to a website listed in the press release. This can help a business rank higher in the search engines through what is called link building.

A press release should have a headline, release date, city, state, and country of origin, media contact information such as name, address, email, fax, and phone number, and in some cases a picture is acceptable on the release.

Modes of Acquisition

Obtaining PR clients can be done in a number of ways. The key to winning press release writing clients starts with having a professional web presence. The type of customers that order press release writing services are not interested in paying a shadowy operation with a minimal and vague website to do their press release writing. Thus, it is imperative to create a website that offers visitors the appearance of a trustworthy, legit, accessible, and timely provider.

This by no means indicates you must go out and pay a bunch of money to some website designer to create a press release writing site for you. Rather, it is more upon you to think about what you can put on a website that makes your service look professional.

Many people that know me will tell you my sites are famously basic. There is almost no flash animation on my website, nor is there any type of sounds, songs, bells, or whistles to be found on any site with my name on it. Nearly all my websites are built off of a simple 5 page template. The key is not how a site is designed, but what is written, and included on a website to build a level of comfort with your visitors.

Your press release writing service website should include an easy way for people to contact you, I recommend live chat via instant messenger or a phone number at which they can call you at. Further your site should offer at least 3 or 4 examples of previous work you have done, and some credentials about your experience as a freelance writer.

Most people that do not have any experience immediately believe they are out of luck when it comes to writing for money. This is not the case; you can easily find people that are willing to pay you nothing, or next to nothing, for you to do writing work for them. By locating these people, and creating a small project of say 3 to 5 different pieces of writing for them, you have in essence gained an acceptable portfolio of samples that can be used on any given website you choose to promote your writing services on.

Most people balk at the idea of writing for free, or little money; however it is one way to build an instant client base, and gain valuable portfolio samples. If you are looking for people that would be willing try your services for little to no money check out the www.WarriorForum.com or http://forums.digitalpoint.com/ for a chance to mingle with amateur freelance business writers and meet people that would easily take you up on a low cost offer. I am not by any means indicating better writing opportunities are not to be found on the above websites, but at the very least, you will find a number of writers in a similar position if you are in fact new to the game, and want to build a portfolio for your upcoming website.

Once your website is up, samples are available, and you are ready to produce quality content for your clients, it is time to market the site. There are plenty of ways this can be done. For starters, you can visit the links above, create an account for free, and market to those people for your writing services. In particular the Warrior Forum is fertile ground for picking up new online writing service clients.

This is how I got my start in freelance writing and marketing online, and while it had nothing to do with producing press releases, the sites are full of people looking for those as well.

Another way to market your service is through search engine marketing, such as Google's AdWords program. This marketing technique is highly rewarding, but also involves a fair amount of risk. Whenever I am mentoring new writers I always advise them to steer clear of this type of marketing unless they have a budget in which they can spend without needing to make any of it back.

I marketed my writing services, including press releases, on the blogs and forums like the two listed above until I had some cash flow to move into search engine marketing. Since I started search engine marketing my business has increased, however there are some days, and even weeks, when the advertising bill greatly outweighs the income brought in.

For more information about search engine marketing I recommend you search Perry Marshall in Google and give his AdWords expert book a read.

Finally press release writing services can be marketed locally. Many providers choose to take this route, as it seems to eliminate any competition. If you are in fact keeping your rates reasonable, chances are there are no other providers in your area calling up local businesses offering a press release writing service for say, $200. This would be a huge amount off the traditional Advertising firm rate card that many of these businesses have probably become familiar with.

WHAT TO EXPECT IN TERMS OF PAY

The going rate for a professional press release is $300. This rate however is hardly what I would recommend charging. The $300 rate is charged by the major PR firm websites that offer this service, and often they discount the price to $200 when someone buys a distribution package from them. That price in my mind is still too high.

I believe the going rate for a single press release is between $75 and $150. This price range has worked best in my marketing efforts, and, if adopted by you, would keep your writing service well under the average price.

Distribution and other aspects of press release services such as editing, and revisions are areas that I am not an expert in, so I would urge you to look at what others are charging, and then charge a bit less on your own website. Remember with distribution that many companies use an established newswire, and that the newswire companies charge fixed rates to publicity firms that if you offered the same service, you would be responsible for paying.

Tips for Getting the Job Done Quickly and Efficiently

Producing a press release is a simple and methodical process. Start by envisioning the headline or lead for the press release, and then go into the body with the lead in mind.

When you sell a press release writing service to individuals you will be sending them a new client information form via email that requests all the pertinent information about their company and corresponding announcement. Using this form, along with a newsy angle, you can create a press release in a matter of hours.

There are dozens of resources online for producing a press release, so I will defer to those resources when it comes to the technicalities of writing a release. My press release writing style can be seen at www.CustomPressRelease.com under the samples page, or at www.DistributionResults.com under the Results page. As you will see from visiting my websites, the style I have for writing press releases is more narrative, and in some cases can be a deterrent from clients. For the most part however, I have found the style to work well for people that purchase a press release from my company.

Disadvantages

The negatives of press release writing are limited. The service is so targeted, and the customer is typically providing the needed information in the new client survey form that you will send them, that major problems are not that prevalent compared to other freelance writing genres.

When an issue does in fact arise, it typically involves a missing component that needs to be included on the release, or some minor or major editing that the client requests to be done. A lot of this depends on your independent research prior to writing the press release to obtain all the information the client wants in the release, as well as the client's ability to be candid about information that needs to be included in the release.

When a pitfall occurs it can usually be remedied through a series of revisions, and often the issue will end. In rare cases a client may in fact ask for a refund, however the rate of client retention with an honest effort is relatively high, and thus refunds stay low as long as you deliver on what you have promised on your website.

The other common problem a press release writer will face is that of newswire editorial rejections. These rejections come from any given newswire service editor that requires changes to be made to a client's press release before it can be distributed. Often this is due to lack of professional appearance, the use of excessive I's, You's, My's, We's and other informal words, overtly promotional material, or lack of company attribution to the headline of the release. Editors of most newswire companies are typically clear in what needs to be fixed, and often the problem can be resolved through a few simple revisions, and a couple of emails to the client and editorial desk of the newswire service the client is using for their press release distribution.

Future Opportunities

Press releases and other ala carte publicity services will remain strong for a longtime to come. With the advent of the Internet, and the online small business, a new breed of low budget, publicity hungry businessmen are on the map, waiting for a provider to present them with a service they can use to promote and expand their business to new heights.

Market Domination Capacity

Market domination is in fact possible for press release writing. There currently is one press release distribution channel online that seems to be far and away the dominate choice for online distribution that is not directly affiliated with a newswire. Therefore it is in theory possible to build an online writing business that is the premier destination for press release writing services. I believe my business is one of the top press release writing businesses on the web, and it took us only about 12 months to get there, so the chance to dominate this market does seem to exist.

Chapter 6
Autoresponder and Email Writing

Email marketing is the most effective and cost efficient method of building a business online. In fact, email marketing is so powerful, that there is an old saying among Internet marketers that has been around as long as the web, the money is in the list. Meaning that the most money can be made from the email list a marketer builds, collects, and sends out messages to on a regular basis.

Most of the projects I work on today are developed specifically for my list of several hundred past freelance writing clients. I did not start out thinking my business would become a virtual catering company to create and market services my email list members could use, however, it has been a lucrative proposition for all involved, so I continue to do it to this day.

I highly advise you to keep your own email list of clients to send writing promotions to in the future. At the very least, you should understand that regardless of what you choose to do with your marketing efforts, the Internet marketing community as a whole puts an extremely high value on email marketing.

From the start of my career online I would record buyers of both my services, and my products email addresses. Even before I went online fulltime as a writer and Internet marketer, I would collect the email addresses of those that visited my boutique downtown, and email them when I had a sale or promotion going on. It was not hard to figure out early on in my career that email marketing is incredibly effective because the cost of entry is so low, and it actually works to bring in sales, and get people to take action.

There is a major angle for writing services within email marketing, but before we venture down that road, let's take a step back and look at how email marketing works.

As you have probably noticed by reading the chapter title email marketing is also referred to as an autoresponder, or autoresponder series. This techno sounding word is so new it's not recognized by my advanced MS WORD spell check. So I do not by any means expect you to have a clue what its definition is, or its purpose. Hey, that's what you got me for, right?

The word autoresponder refers to a piece of software, often hosted online, that delivers email messages to a subscription list on cue. The autoresponder will often deliver a series of messages in a preformatted fashion to a subscriber's inbox, typically done in 5, 10, or even 20 day increments.

Here is where the writing comes into play. An autoresponder is typically used to break the ice with a potential buyer of a product or service. Most often when sales leads visit a website, they are encouraged to enter their name and email address into a small box that in turn sends the information to the autoresponder, which in turn sends out a series of messages. These messages offer helpful tips about the subject matter of the website, and in the end urge the recipient of the messages to take action and buy a certain product or service. This form of daily automated marketing is called an autoresponder series.

Freelance writers are often commissioned to produce compelling autoresponder series emails for clients that are interested in breaking the ice with their leads, building a level of comfort, and eventually selling them something.

As with most of my online writing exploits, this particular genre of online writing came to me accidentally. I was in the process of promoting my own e-book on ways to make money online via my own autoresponder email series which consisted of a whopping 2 days of emails, when I received a surprise response from a list member.

The member of one of my small email lists had read my offer for the new e-book, was not interested in buying the e-book, but felt that the way the email was written was compelling enough to him, that he wanted me to create an email series for his product.

Which of course I agreed to do, got paid a few hundred bucks, and enjoyed the process.

Anytime someone approaches me about a unique online writing job, I have to take a step back, and think about what other people might want when it comes to this new service. At the time I did not know how popular an autoresponder series is in the online Internet marketing world. After several years in the game I can assure you this is an incredible and essential part of most online marketer's campaigns, and thus remains absolutely in demand.

So there is probably a million people writing these autoresponder series emails as freelancers, right? Wrong. In fact, most people end up doing these autoresponder emails on their own because they cannot find any experts in the field to do it for them.

While some forms of online writing ventures face formidable competition, such as press release writing, the area of autoresponder writing is so wide open, it hardly exists today as a market. Prime domain names remain available, few businesses offer this service, and the freelance writers smart enough to position themselves as experts have, in my opinion, become greedy with their rates and terms. All of the above elements make this a ripe market for an online freelance writer like you to profit from.

Definition

Email writing or autoresponder writing can be defined as a small piece of informal sales material that is used to prime and pre-sell a potential buyer on a product or service. Emails are typically delivered in a daily fashion for a number of days as small as 1 and as great as 365. An autoresponder program is typically used to deliver the emails to a targeted email list. Popular programs include Aweber, Icontact, and Constant Contact.

Modes of Acquisition

Obtaining autoresponder writing business is most likely to occur through package deals with custom e-book creation, or on freelance job boards such as Elance.com or Guru.com. One can also try to obtain new business through search engine marketing and forum marketing as well.

Autoresponder series clients can also be found through discovering the publishers of popular e-books, and other downloadable items. Typically those that sell and market an e-book will offer an autoresponder series to clients, and thus may be in the process of creating a new product, which in turn might need an autoresponder series to help sell it. Also, these publishers might agree to allow one to produce new or revised versions of an underperforming autoresponder series.

WHAT TO EXPECT IN TERMS OF PAY

Rates for this type of work are hard to define. Typically one would charge the client on a per day basis. If the autoresponder series was to be 5 days long, the service provider would charge the client a daily rate multiplied by 5 for the project. It is also important to define a word count per day, as some clients may envision a daily email much longer than others.

Rates for this work are often bundled with e-book projects, and other online freelance writing jobs. It is for this reason that the market is so wide open one can literally define their own price per day without having to deal with much competition when it comes to price.

I currently charge $10 per day for one of my junior writers to produce the content, which has converted fairly well. There could be rates higher or lower than mine and it still would probably work out fine with clients as there is no real market rate other than what the client has budgeted for a particular project.

TIPS FOR GETTING THE JOB DONE QUICKLY AND EFFICIENTLY

Producing an autoresponder series for a client is a 3-step process. One must first identify what the client's primary objective for the series of emails is. Once a primary objective has been established, one can identify the actual length of the email series by both words, and days, and then start the writing process.

The final step in creating an autoresponder series is making sure the entire series when read through chronologically does its job. If the client's primary objective is to sell a diet supplement pill, then at the end of the final day of the autoresponder email series the reader should be left with little doubt, and plenty of motivation to visit the client's site and purchase the diet pill.

Essentially an autoresponder email series is nothing more than an educational form of a sales letter that subtly pushes a lead in the direction of taking action. Producing an autoresponder email series with this in mind will help you keep your clients happy, and help your business grow as your current clients refer your services to others in need of autoresponder series email writing.

DISADVANTAGES

What to watch out for when producing autoresponder emails primarily depends on the nature of the product or service you are tasked with writing about. Some clients prefer hard selling emails that focus entirely on the product or service they are trying to sell. Other clients wish to educate their potential customers and offer as much value as possible.

As you can see from the two likely scenarios above, it is important to discuss expectations and overall details of the autoresponder series that is about to be produced with the client before the creation process occurs. This will lower your chances of upsetting a client with the final product, and raise the chances of pleasing a client with the final product.

Other risks with producing autoresponder emails include not knowing a product or service well enough to effectively sell it via email, not buying into what the client wants you to push to the lead into buying, not being able to produce enough content for the allotted days in the email series requested and not being able to sell a product or service simply because it is not up to snuff with market standards. All of these risks can be prevented by performing a brisk presale analysis with a potential client before accepting payment or a deposit for the job.

FUTURE OPPORTUNITIES

Things are looking up for the autoresponder series. While there are increasingly more emails coming into people's inboxes, and many more spam messages among them, for the most part email marketing remains ideal and effective for most online businesses.

Therefore, it is a bright and sunny forecast for those writing autoresponder emails for clients. With such as lack of qualified providers at the moment, those that work to get a foothold in the market should be able to keep their plates full with jobs for a longtime to come.

Market Domination Capacity

Since autoresponder email series writing is such a niche service, market domination is absolutely possible. There are simply too few providers to compete with not to have a shot at dominating this underserved market. A persuasive website, a large offering of past client testimonials, and robust portfolio of work will help ensure market domination in this new and growing online freelance writing field.

Chapter 7
Blogs

Writing blog posts is yet another lucrative way to earn money on the Internet. There are literally hundreds of thousands of blogs on the net today, many of which are in dire need of fresh content. The art of paid blog posting is as old as the blog itself, with many notable big name corporations hiring full and part time blog posters to their staff only adds credibility to this unique writing gig.

As a green freelance writer still in the process of quitting my various teaching jobs, I was instantly enticed to the market of blog posting jobs due to the low amount of words needed, and the fun, and often whimsical style of writing known simply as blogging.

While I wish I could sit here and tell you that my first blog writing gig was a glamorous assignment covering celebrities on the red carpet, or interviewing professional athletes after a big game, in reality it was a nothing more than a tips to quit smoking blog. The blog was owned by a company that made herbal nicotine patches, and thus they were interested in promoting their product through cleverly written tips to quit smoking in an easy to access blog format.

For $50 a week I would post a 300 to 500 word blog article Monday through Friday on the various tricks and tips to quitting smoking. The blog topic was simple, the pay was decent, and the client was very friendly. All of this added up to a pleasant experience that I am glad to have partaken in. The blog only lasted a few months, since the budget was tight, but in those few months a new industry for freelance writers was showcased, an industry that to this day is so wide open, it would be a shame not to dedicate at least 1 chapter to discussing it.

Definition

Blog posting or blogging as it is commonly referred to, is the simple art of writing an online journal entry publishable upon a single push of a button. Blog posts tend to be short, often include hyperlinks to other websites, and are usually accompanied with media such as photos, videos, audio recordings, and on occasion a mesh of all the above.

Modes of Acquisition

Paid posting for blog jobs is typically found on freelance boards such as Elance.com and Guru.com, as well as on websites such as http://jobs.problogger.net which lists a current database of open blog related jobs.

What to Expect in Terms of Pay

Blog posting jobs vary greatly in the pay offered and the terms of the job. Fulltime blog posting jobs offered by established companies can pay upwards of fifty thousand dollars per year, while pay per post jobs such as my experience above, pay anywhere from $1 to $40 per post. On average a poster should expect to be paid at least few dollars per post, and if they are getting anything over $10 per post it would be considered a fairly good situation.

There is revenue sharing services that offer bloggers a percentage of the advertising earnings made from their blog posts. These services typically pay a few cents per post per day based on the topic, often these services rely heavily on passionate writers that do not mind low pay for an opportunity to get the word out about their passion.

For more information on revenue sharing blog posting gigs check out one of the larger blog networks out there http://www.b5media.com.

Finally those that create, and develop a blog can receive payments per post from online review companies that sell blog reviews to advertisers. This can be a lucrative way to make money off of a blog; however the blog must have some type of traffic, and often needs to be a certain age to qualify.

For more information on the pay per post review style concept check out one of the leading websites in the industry http://pay-perpost.com.

Tips for Getting the Job Done Quickly and Efficiently

Posting to blogs is typically an easy assignment compared to most freelance writing gigs. The format is typically freestyle, without too much consideration for AP, APA, or MLA style. Further, citations for blogs are often optional, and the use of photographs can help illustrate a story without the use of excessive descriptions. While all blogs vary in their context and requirements, most blog posting is in the spirit of an online journal entry that will interest others in a short, brief, to the point article format.

Disadvantages

Blogs by nature are written often on a whim, and thus misinformation can often end up on a live published blog post. Further, blogs are often stuffed with media like pictures, audio files, and YouTube style videos; if a hosted file becomes unavailable your blog post might look somewhat odd. To help curb these issues, check facts before posting, and host all your media files that are going to be used in your posts on your own computer.

Future Opportunities

Blogs seem to be as hot as ever, and will continue to evolve into multimedia platforms of video, audio, and the written word. Blogs have a bright future, and thus blog post writing should also. Those that invest in learning new technologies like digital video will have an edge over those that choose to stick to the written word.

Market Domination Capacity

Becoming the go-to blog posting expert is unlikely due to the wide variety of topics that blogs encompass on the net. That however does not mean, that one could not own a company with a team of writers that offered relative blog content on say the most popular 20 blog topics. The market is underserved with qualified writers, and qualified blog posting businesses. If one is able to get the word out about their blog posting service, the rates are kept competitive; blog posting in a niche market could absolutely be dominated by one writer, or a team of writers.

Chapter 8
Newsletter Writing and Design

2007 was all about me coming out of my freelance writer shell, at least it was a series of attempts at this somewhat hard to obtain feat. My life up to that point was largely encompassed with writing. No matter how many team members I added, or how many projects I outsourced, it still seemed that the bulk of work I would handle in a day was all about writing.

I would write press releases, sales letters, and an article here and there and of course the content for my growing flock of websites that were used to promote my services. While I found it therapeutic to write, similar to the way one feels after a two mile jog around town, it was secretly eating away at my productivity. It took most of '07 for me to realize this, after all my income went from a modest $50 to $100 per day to upwards of $300 to $500 per day and growing rapidly. Still, I knew if I wanted to get over the impending productivity hump my business was about to face, I had to change course. I had to work less in the business, and more on the business. I had to increase the per page rate for work my team could do, without having to actually write the content myself if my team fell short. All of this leads to a weekend long stint as the official camera guy for a real estate investor's conference that surprisingly led to a useful insight into the growing demand for newsletter producers.

Do I have any camera skills whatsoever you might be wondering? No, I do not. I can't even keep the darn thing steady. My better half Elizabeth is a wonderful camera operator, anything she films or takes a picture of turns into a work of art. Me on the other hand, I have trouble keeping the camera from wobbling in my hands... heck I have trouble standing still. All that said, I was graciously invited to a secret real estate investor conference by one of my freelance writing clients to film the event.

The theory my client had was that if I were able to film the event, I would learn much more about his style of real estate investing, and then in essence be better prepared to write a sales letter that would captivate visitors to take action and buy his product when they visited his website. Truth be told my weekend in the camera guy business was a lot of fun, and I hardly changed a word on that sales letter after the fact, as it was written more from the perspective of the client's personal struggle to succeed than it was on the intricacies of the event itself.

At this weekend long event I met a guy that was getting out of the business, he seemed to have a false sense of security about his new profession, seminar speaker, and needed a newsletter to gel everything together for his first upcoming "educational" seminar. He wanted me to write it.

After discussing his need for a monthly newsletter via several conversations on the phone throughout the next week I realized two things, first the client was desperate, and second the client was clueless about what it takes to produce a newsletter. To him it just seemed like the right thing to do, like something he was advised of in his marketing 101 textbook.

Although I am sad to report the client stopped calling after I quoted him a five figure rate for his newsletter, I did learn one thing from the situation, newsletter writing is a service that is not readily available, and is absolutely in demand.

I can only infer that big time companies like Coca Cola or Starbucks would have their newsletters, even the internal one for employees, done by a major marketing or PR firm. The only other option would be to have the newsletters created by a staff member for the company. Both options are viable and probably best practices for this type of thing, but what about the business owner that does not have the budget to hire a large marketing firm? What about the business owner that does not have the resources to have an employee do the newsletter each month? Where do they get their services from? The answer is, they don't.

Doing a quick search on the Internet for what I think might be the best phrase to fit this need, newsletter content, I found very few businesses offering affordable writing and design services. Mostly what you will uncover is template-based newsletters available for purchase. Stale information from old articles and cookie cutter newsletter templates seem to be available for sale in mass amounts. Leaving the market wide open for any writer willing to match the price of the old stuff, and offer new custom creation instead.

Definition

Newsletter content is best defined as the written words inside a newsletter that include stories, tid-bits, fast facts, jokes, did you know information, valuable time saving information, nutritional information and so on. Most newsletters are written from a value-driven perspective. The conventional wisdom is that if a newsletter delivers a valuable set of informative articles and blurbs, it can in effect soft sell the reader into taking action on buying a service or product.

Newsletter design is the layout and graphic structure of the newsletter. Design elements can include pictures, clipart, cartoons, graphs and charts, and a wide variety of column based formats. Newsletter design is often catered to the format of delivery. If a newsletter is being distributed electronically it most likely will be designed in a HTML format, whereas if a newsletter is being designed for print delivery it can be done in DOC, PDF, PSD, and other print friendly formats.

A newsletter is often distributed monthly, although newsletters can be distributed weekly, biweekly, quarterly, yearly, or whenever the organization chooses to deliver it.

While the Internet has popularized electronic newsletters, there has always been a great demand for print newsletters, as spam and junk mail continue to clog user's inboxes; the trend towards print newsletters continues to grow, as there is often less mail to compete with on the printed format than the electronic delivery format.

Finally newsletters can often take the shape of basic email messages, similar to what was discussed in the autoresponder chapter, as the word newsletter is used loosely online often in an effort to gain a new email list subscriber for promotional purposes.

Modes of Acquisition

This genre of freelance online writing has typically been limited to the freelance job boards such as Guru.com and Elance.com. While there have been some standalone websites, for the most part the business acquired was from word of mouth, or bids placed on online job board projects from my experience.

Through a series of tests, I have determined there is absolutely a market for a website based service that is marketed through pay per click advertising. However, the site I created to cater to this market, NewsletterContent.Net is only fairing so well, as the interested people that click on this advertisement rarely take action resulting in a relatively high cost of acquisition through pay per click marketing.

With a website, a membership to the popular online job boards one should be able to obtain a fair amount of work in this field without dealing with too much competition.

What to Expect in Terms of Pay

There is no real price structure for newsletter writing gigs. One can charge a high rate of $100 or more per page, or one can charge a fixed rate of just $10 per page, or anything in between that mark. Through my testing the $97 for about 6 pages of writing seems to convert well, however you will need to deal with the design aspect as it is my experience client's are not pleased with a basic MS Word document delivery. They want a preformatted, ready to ship design to the newsletter.

Tips for Getting the Job Done Quickly and Efficiently

Producing newsletters is fairly simple; the main element of getting it done involves creating a quick organizational chart before writing. The chart should address each function of the newsletter such as value, selling, promotional offers, and so on, while at the same time allow the content to fall into your basic newsletter format.

While there is no expert on newsletter format that I know of, it seems that a feature story, several smaller stories, and a few tidbit facts work best for a basic newsletter. For more information on the format my company uses for producing newsletters visit our site www.NewsletterContent.Net.

Disadvantages

The major problem with newsletter production is letting the client down with no design aspects. Our core business is producing content, thus it is hard for us to produce graphical templates to put the newsletters into on a regular basis, and thus this particular writing job is not an easy one. That said, demand is high for newsletter production, and investing in some templates probably makes a lot of sense. The major pitfall in my experience thus far is design, and also content creation, since many clients will expect big marketing firm service for whatever price they are paying. That means longer stories that deliver excellent value to the end reader.

Future Opportunities

Newsletters seem to be an absolute steady market for the foreseeable future. There are simply too many small businesses that cannot afford big time marketing firm retainers that are in dire need of newsletters. Even after pulling the online ads for our service we still received several new clients based solely on the fact that they have been in need of such a service for years. It is for this reason that newsletter jobs will maintain popularity in the freelance writing business for a longtime to come. The question is how will you cater your service to meet the budgetary, design, and custom content needs of your future clients? Answering that question thoroughly will give your business the optimal chance to succeed.

Market Domination Capacity

Dominating the newsletter content creation market is absolutely possible since so few marketers and writers are offering such a service online. Most big time marketing firms rely on ambiguous websites that offer nothing more than flash animation and clichés about marketing and visibility, thus leaving the market ripe for writers that build websites that cut to the chase, and offer a clear menu of services with reasonable prices and most importantly a place to sign up.

Chapter 9
A Few Other Jobs

Ok I admit it; we did not cover every single market of online writing in this book. It fell a bit short, there are a few other jobs out there that probably don't yet deserve a chapter in a book like this, but for the sake of being thorough and giving you all the options when it comes to writing for profit online, here are a few other online writing markets that are a worth a look.

Product Descriptions

As more and more companies bring their products online through ecommerce websites, the demand for product descriptions continues to increase. This is the perfect team oriented job, as often the big money is only made in doing a large sum of short, to the point descriptions of products.

Our company has been fortunate enough to have worked on product descriptions for major retailers in such diverse fields as gift basket arrangements, lingerie, remote controlled cars, wedding favors, candles, log cabin furniture, and vitamin supplements to name a few.

A product description is often found below or to the side of a particular product's picture in an ecommerce store. The description usually ranges from a few words to a few hundred words, and often is a dual attempt to inform the shopper about a product's features, while at the same time attempting to persuade the shopper to purchase.

Writing product descriptions is particularly easy since most clients will provide a list of specs for each product, and a picture or series of pictures to review before writing the description.

The rates for writing product descriptions range, however since most people outsourcing this type of work are in need of a large quantity of descriptions, I typically charge between $1 and $3 per description. This equals out to about 5 descriptions per page, which would net a per page rate average of around $10.

Product description work is typically found on freelance boards such as Elance.com and Guru.com. Some of our product description work is displayed at our web content site under the samples tab; you can check it out at www.WebCopywritingService.com.

Rewrites

A popular and cheap way to buy original content is to pay a writer to rewrite existing content. Rewriting is a science more than art. It is often done paragraph by paragraph through calculated paraphrasing of words and sentences.

Before you go calling the plagiarism police, realize that rewriting is often done on basic SEO style articles that are most likely not copyrighted, and often are sold with the right to alter. This gives the client the full authority to pay for a writer to rewrite the content as original. As sketchy as this style of writing sounds, it is very popular, and is often sold for, I hope you are sitting down, $3 to $4 per page. That chump change is not exactly ideal for the freelance writer looking to make a million, but in exchange for a cheap per page rate, many clients will forward hundreds, and in some cases, thousands of pages of content to a provider that has proven they can get it done.

Rewriting jobs are typically found in the places where Internet marketers hangout such as the Warrior Forum, or Digital Point, or Sitepoint.

Rewriting jobs are often delegated to people overseas, to cheap labor, or to anyone that is in need of cash and does not mind working long hours to make it.

You can check out a site I have with one of my partner's Todd Taylor at www.PLRadvantage.com for more information about the rewriting business, and how it is done.

AND YET A FEW MORE

It seems like the list of writing opportunities on the Internet could go on for a thousand pages. There are just too many websites and online projects coming out of the woodwork today for there not to be a ton of writing opportunities online. Some of the other notable opportunities that I have yet to explore, and that we as a company have yet to do anything with, is that of whitepaper writing, technical writing, research reports, grant writing, resume writing, academic writing and editing, fiction related ghostwriting, romantic and adult content writing, fan fiction writing, journalistic writing, and foreign language translational writing. There is no doubt great writing opportunities that are not listed here as well, which goes to show you just how much opportunity there is for a freelance writer that chooses to market and produce content for the online crowd.

Conclusion

Congratulations, you can now call yourself an expert in the online freelance writing market. This information hopefully will help you succeed in your writing endeavors. In fact, if you use it wisely, I know it will.

There have been many topics discussed in this book, so I want to urge you to take a deep breath, and review each chapter again before building out your websites or going too far into your marketing campaigns. These chapters will serve you well, as they are my true life experience with each genre of online freelance writing campaigns.

I am sure there will be things you have questions about in this book, so feel free to contact me at the email address below. If you enjoyed the book, I'd love to hear from you as well. One of my plans for the future of this e-book is to build an online testimonial page with links to my reader's websites that they have constructed by being inspired through this book. So whether you have a question, comment, or just want to pass on some words of encouragement, or criticism, feel free to email me at the address below.

TalkToClark@gmail.com

All Rights Reserved Copyright 2008 Rufus Space Industries, INC.